ALTO SAX

101 BROADWAY SONGS

Available for
FLUTE, CLARINET, ALTO SAX, TENOR SAX, TRUMPET,
HORN, TROMBONE, VIOLIN, VIOLA, CELLO

ISBN 978-1-4950-5248-4

HAL•LEONARD® CORPORATION
7777 W. BLUEMOUND RD. P.O. BOX 13819 MILWAUKEE, WI 53213

CONTENTS

ALL I ASK OF YOU
from THE PHANTOM OF THE OPERA

ALTO SAX

Music by ANDREW LLOYD WEBBER
Lyrics by CHARLES HART
Additional Lyrics by RICHARD STILGOE

ANY DREAM WILL DO

from JOSEPH AND THE AMAZING TECHNICOLOR® DREAMCOAT

ALTO SAX

Music by ANDREW LLOYD WEBBER
Lyrics by TIM RICE

ANYTHING YOU CAN DO

from the Stage Production ANNIE GET YOUR GUN

ALTO SAX

Words and Music by
IRVING BERLIN

As If We Never Said Goodbye

from SUNSET BOULEVARD

ALTO SAX

Music by ANDREW LLOYD WEBBER
Lyrics by DON BLACK and CHRISTOPHER HAMPTON,
with contributions by AMY POWERS

AS LONG AS HE NEEDS ME

from the Broadway Musical OLIVER!

ALTO SAX

Words and Music by
LIONEL BART

BALI HA'I
from SOUTH PACIFIC

ALTO SAX

Lyrics by OSCAR HAMMERSTEIN II
Music by RICHARD RODGERS

BAUBLES, BANGLES AND BEADS

from KISMET

ALTO SAX

Words and Music by ROBERT WRIGHT
and GEORGE FORREST
(Music Based on Themes of A. BORODIN)

BROTHERHOOD OF MAN
from HOW TO SUCCEED IN BUSINESS WITHOUT REALLY TRYING

ALTO SAX

By FRANK LOESSER

CABARET
from the Musical CABARET

ALTO SAX

Words by FRED EBB
Music by JOHN KANDER

CAN'T TAKE MY EYES OFF OF YOU

featured in JERSEY BOYS

ALTO SAX

Words and Music by BOB CREWE
and BOB GAUDIO

CIRCLE OF LIFE

Disney Presents THE LION KING: THE BROADWAY MUSICAL

ALTO SAX

Music by ELTON JOHN
Lyrics by TIM RICE

Moderately, with an African beat

CLIMB EV'RY MOUNTAIN
from THE SOUND OF MUSIC

ALTO SAX

Lyrics by OSCAR HAMMERSTEIN II
Music by RICHARD RODGERS

CLOSE EVERY DOOR

from JOSEPH AND THE AMAZING TECHNICOLOR® DREAMCOAT

ALTO SAX

Music by ANDREW LLOYD WEBBER
Lyrics by TIM RICE

Moderately, expressively

DANCING QUEEN

from MAMMA MIA!

ALTO SAX

Words and Music by BENNY ANDERSSON,
BJÖRN ULVAEUS and STIG ANDERSON

DEFYING GRAVITY
from the Broadway Musical WICKED

ALTO SAX

Music and Lyrics by
STEPHEN SCHWARTZ

Tempo I

DO-RE-MI
from THE SOUND OF MUSIC

ALTO SAX

Lyrics by OSCAR HAMMERSTEIN II
Music by RICHARD RODGERS

DO YOU HEAR THE PEOPLE SING?

from LES MISÉRABLES

Alto Sax

Music by CLAUDE-MICHEL SCHÖNBERG
Lyrics by ALAIN BOUBLIL, JEAN-MARC NATEL
and HERBERT KRETZMER

DON'T CRY FOR ME ARGENTINA

from EVITA

ALTO SAX

Words by TIM RICE
Music by ANDREW LLOYD WEBBER

EASTER PARADE

from AS THOUSANDS CHEER

ALTO SAX

Words and Music by
IRVING BERLIN

Moderately

EDELWEISS
from THE SOUND OF MUSIC

ALTO SAX

Lyrics by OSCAR HAMMERSTEIN II
Music by RICHARD RODGERS

EVERYTHING'S ALRIGHT

from JESUS CHRIST SUPERSTAR

ALTO SAX

Words by TIM RICE
Music by ANDREW LLOYD WEBBER

A FOGGY DAY (IN LONDON TOWN)

from A DAMSEL IN DISTRESS

ALTO SAX

Music and Lyrics by GEORGE GERSHWIN
and IRA GERSHWIN

GETTING TO KNOW YOU

from THE KING AND I

ALTO SAX

Lyrics by OSCAR HAMMERSTEIN II
Music by RICHARD RODGERS

FRIEND LIKE ME
(Stageplay Version)
from the Walt Disney Stageplay ALADDIN

ALTO SAX

Music by ALAN MENKEN
Lyrics by HOWARD ASHMAN
and STEPHEN SCHWARTZ

GUYS AND DOLLS
from GUYS AND DOLLS

ALTO SAX

By FRANK LOESSER

HELLO, DOLLY!

from HELLO, DOLLY!

ALTO SAX

Music and Lyric by
JERRY HERMAN

HOME

from Walt Disney's BEAUTY AND THE BEAST: THE BROADWAY MUSICAL

ALTO SAX

Music by ALAN MENKEN
Lyrics by TIM RICE

HOW ARE THINGS IN GLOCCA MORRA

from FINIAN'S RAINBOW

ALTO SAX

Words by E.Y. "YIP" HARBURG
Music by BURTON LANE

I BELIEVE IN YOU
from HOW TO SUCCEED IN BUSINESS WITHOUT REALLY TRYING

ALTO SAX

By FRANK LOESSER

I DON'T KNOW HOW TO LOVE HIM
from JESUS CHRIST SUPERSTAR

ALTO SAX

Words by TIM RICE
Music by ANDREW LLOYD WEBBER

Slowly, expressively

I DREAMED A DREAM
from LES MISÉRABLES

ALTO SAX

Music by CLAUDE-MICHEL SCHÖNBERG
Lyrics by ALAIN BOUBLIL, JEAN-MARC NATEL
and HERBERT KRETZMER

I GOT PLENTY O' NUTTIN'

from PORGY AND BESS®

ALTO SAX

Music and Lyrics by GEORGE GERSHWIN,
DuBOSE and DORTHY HEYWARD
and IRA GERSHWIN

I WHISTLE A HAPPY TUNE

from THE KING AND I

ALTO SAX

Lyrics by OSCAR HAMMERSTEIN II
Music by RICHARD RODGERS

Brightly

I'VE NEVER BEEN IN LOVE BEFORE

from GUYS AND DOLLS

ALTO SAX

By FRANK LOESSER

IF I LOVED YOU

from CAROUSEL

ALTO SAX

Lyrics by OSCAR HAMMERSTEIN II
Music by RICHARD RODGERS

Slowly

IF I WERE A BELL
from GUYS AND DOLLS

ALTO SAX

By FRANK LOESSER

IF I WERE A RICH MAN

from the Musical FIDDLER ON THE ROOF

ALTO SAX

Words by SHELDON HARNICK
Music by JERRY BOCK

THE IMPOSSIBLE DREAM
(The Quest)
from MAN OF LA MANCHA

ALTO SAX

Lyric by JOE DARION
Music by MITCH LEIGH

IT AIN'T NECESSARILY SO

from PORGY AND BESS®

Alto Sax

Music and Lyrics by GEORGE GERSHWIN,
DuBOSE and DOROTHY HEYWARD
and IRA GERSHWIN

THE LADY IS A TRAMP
from BABES IN ARMS

ALTO SAX

Words by LORENZ HART
Music by RICHARD RODGERS

THE LAST NIGHT OF THE WORLD

from MISS SAIGON

ALTO SAX

Music by CLAUDE-MICHEL SCHÖNBERG
Lyrics by ALAIN BOUBLIL and RICHARD MALTBY JR.
Adapted from original French Lyrics by ALAIN BOUBLIL

LET'S CALL THE WHOLE THING OFF

from SHALL WE DANCE

ALTO SAX

Music and Lyrics by GEORGE GERSHWIN
and IRA GERSHWIN

LOVE IS HERE TO STAY
from GOLDWYN FOLLIES

ALTO SAX

Music and Lyrics by GEORGE GERSHWIN
and IRA GERSHWIN

LOVE ME OR LEAVE ME

from WHOOPEE!

ALTO SAX

Lyrics by GUS KAHN
Music by WALTER DONALDSON

LOVE WALKED IN
from GOLDWYN FOLLIES

ALTO SAX

Music and Lyrics by GEORGE GERSHWIN
and IRA GERSHWIN

LUCK BE A LADY
from GUYS AND DOLLS

ALTO SAX

By FRANK LOESSER

MAKIN' WHOOPEE!

from WHOOPEE!

ALTO SAX

Lyrics by GUS KAHN
Music by WALTER DONALDSON

MAME

from MAME

ALTO SAX

Music and Lyric by
JERRY HERMAN

MAMMA MIA

from MAMMA MIA!

ALTO SAX

Words and Music by BENNY ANDERSSON,
BJÖRN ULVAEUS and STIG ANDERSON

MATCHMAKER
from the Musical FIDDLER ON THE ROOF

ALTO SAX

Words by SHELDON HARNICK
Music by JERRY BOCK

MAYBE

from the Musical Production ANNIE

ALTO SAX

Lyric by MARTIN CHARNIN
Music by CHARLES STROUSE

MEMORY
from CATS

ALTO SAX

Music by ANDREW LLOYD WEBBER
Text by TREVOR NUNN after T.S. ELIOT

THE MUSIC OF THE NIGHT

from THE PHANTOM OF THE OPERA

ALTO SAX

Music by ANDREW LLOYD WEBBER
Lyrics by CHARLES HART
Additional Lyrics by RICHARD STILGOE

MY FAVORITE THINGS
from THE SOUND OF MUSIC

ALTO SAX

Lyrics by OSCAR HAMMERSTEIN II
Music by RICHARD RODGERS

Lively, with spirit

NICE WORK IF YOU CAN GET IT

from A DAMSEL IN DISTRESS

ALTO SAX

Music and Lyrics by GEORGE GERSHWIN
and IRA GERSWIN

OH, WHAT A BEAUTIFUL MORNIN'

from OKLAHOMA!

ALTO SAX

Lyrics by OSCAR HAMMERSTEIN II
Music by RICHARD RODGERS

OKLAHOMA
from OKLAHOMA!

ALTO SAX

Lyrics by OSCAR HAMMERSTEIN II
Music by RICHARD RODGERS

OL' MAN RIVER

from SHOW BOAT

ALTO SAX

Lyrics by OSCAR HAMMERSTEIN II
Music by JEROME KERN

OLD DEVIL MOON
from FINIAN'S RAINBOW

Alto Sax

Words by E.Y. "YIP" HARBURG
Music by BURTON LANE

ON MY OWN
from LES MISÉRABLES

ALTO SAX

Music by CLAUDE-MICHEL SCHÖNBERG
Lyrics by ALAIN BOUBLIL, JEAN-MARC NATEL,
HERBERT KRETZMER, JOHN CAIRD
and TREVOR NUNN

Music and French Lyrics Copyright © 1980 by Editions Musicales Alain Boublil
English Lyrics Copyright © 1986 by Alain Boublil Music Ltd. (ASCAP)
Mechanical and Publication Rights for the U.S.A. Administered by Alain Boublil Music Ltd. (ASCAP) c/o Spielman Koenigsberg & Parker LLP,
Richard Koenigsberg, 1745 Broadway, New York NY 10019, Tel 212-453-2500, Fax 212-453-2550, ABML@skpny.com

ONCE IN A LIFETIME

from the Musical Production STOP THE WORLD—I WANT TO GET OFF

ALTO SAX

Words and Music by LESLIE BRICUSSE
and ANTHONY NEWLEY

ONCE IN LOVE WITH AMY

from WHERE'S CHARLEY?

ALTO SAX

By FRANK LOESSER

ONE
from A CHORUS LINE

ALTO SAX

Music by MARVIN HAMLISCH
Lyric by EDWARD KLEBAN

PEOPLE WILL SAY WE'RE IN LOVE

from OKLAHOMA!

ALTO SAX

Lyrics by OSCAR HAMMERSTEIN II
Music by RICHARD RODGERS

THE PHANTOM OF THE OPERA
from THE PHANTOM OF THE OPERA

ALTO SAX

Music by ANDREW LLOYD WEBBER
Lyrics by CHARLES HART
Additional Lyrics by RICHARD STILGOE
and MIKE BATT

POPULAR
from the Broadway Musical WICKED

ALTO SAX

Music and Lyrics by
STEPHEN SCHWARTZ

SEASONS OF LOVE

from RENT

ALTO SAX

Words and Music by
JONATHAN LARSON

Moderately

SEND IN THE CLOWNS
from the Musical A LITTLE NIGHT MUSIC

ALTO SAX

Words and Music by
STEPHEN SONDHEIM

SEVENTY SIX TROMBONES

from Meredith Willson's THE MUSIC MAN

ALTO SAX

By MEREDITH WILLSON

SHALL WE DANCE?
from THE KING AND I

ALTO SAX

Lyrics by OSCAR HAMMERSTEIN II
Music by RICHARD RODGERS

SHE LOVES ME

from SHE LOVES ME

ALTO SAX

Words by SHELDON HARNICK
Music by JERRY BOCK

SHERRY
featured in JERSEY BOYS

ALTO SAX

Words and Music by
BOB GAUDIO

SOME ENCHANTED EVENING

from SOUTH PACIFIC

ALTO SAX

Lyrics by OSCAR HAMMERSTEIN II
Music by RICHARD RODGERS

SUMMERTIME
from PORGY AND BESS®

ALTO SAX

Music and Lyrics by GEORGE GERSHWIN,
DuBOSE and DOROTHY HEYWARD
and IRA GERSHWIN

SUNRISE, SUNSET

from the Musical FIDDLER ON THE ROOF

ALTO SAX

Words by SHELDON HARNICK
Music by JERRY BOCK

SUPERSTAR
from JESUS CHRIST SUPERSTAR

ALTO SAX

Words by TIM RICE
Music by ANDREW LLOYD WEBBER

THE SURREY WITH THE FRINGE ON TOP

from OKLAHOMA!

ALTO SAX

Lyrics by OSCAR HAMMERSTEIN II
Music by RICHARD RODGERS

THE SWEETEST SOUNDS

from NO STRINGS

ALTO SAX

Lyrics and Music by
RICHARD RODGERS

Moderately

THERE'S NO BUSINESS LIKE SHOW BUSINESS

from the Stage Production ANNIE GET YOUR GUN

ALTO SAX

Words and Music by
IRVING BERLIN

THEY ALL LAUGHED

from SHALL WE DANCE

ALTO SAX

Music and Lyrics by GEORGE GERSHWIN
and IRA GERSHWIN

THEY CAN'T TAKE THAT AWAY FROM ME

from SHALL WE DANCE

ALTO SAX

Music and Lyrics by GEORGE GERSHWIN
and IRA GERSHWIN

THINK OF ME

from THE PHANTOM OF THE OPERA

ALTO SAX

Music by ANDREW LLOYD WEBBER
Lyrics by CHARLES HART
Additional Lyrics by RICHARD STILGOE

THIS IS THE MOMENT
from JEKYLL & HYDE

ALTO SAX

Words and Music by LESLIE BRICUSSE
and FRANK WILDHORN

THIS NEARLY WAS MINE
from SOUTH PACIFIC

ALTO SAX

Lyrics by OSCAR HAMMERSTEIN II
Music by RICHARD RODGERS

TILL THERE WAS YOU
from Meredith Willson's THE MUSIC MAN

ALTO SAX

By MEREDITH WILLSON

TOMORROW
from the Musical Production ANNIE

ALTO SAX

Lyric by MARTIN CHARNIN
Music by CHARLES STROUSE

WALK LIKE A MAN

featured in JERSEY BOYS

ALTO SAX

Words and Music by BOB CREWE
and BOB GAUDIO

UNUSUAL WAY
from NINE

ALTO SAX

Music and Lyrics by
MAURY YESTON

WHAT I DID FOR LOVE

from A CHORUS LINE

ALTO SAX

Music by MARVIN HAMLISCH
Lyric by EDWARD KLEBAN

WHAT KIND OF FOOL AM I?

from the Musical Production STOP THE WORLD—I WANT TO GET OFF

ALTO SAX

Words and Music by LESLIE BRICUSSE
and ANTHONY NEWLEY

WHERE IS LOVE?

from the Broadway Musical OLIVER!

ALTO SAX

Words and Music by
LIONEL BART

WHO CAN I TURN TO
(When Nobody Needs Me)
from THE ROAR OF THE GREASEPAINT—THE SMELL OF THE CROWD

Alto Sax

Words and Music by LESLIE BRICUSSE
and ANTHONY NEWLEY

A WHOLE NEW WORLD

from the Walt Disney Stageplay ALADDIN

ALTO SAX

Music by ALAN MENKEN
Lyrics by TIM RICE

Moderately

WILL YOU LOVE ME TOMORROW
(Will You Still Love Me Tomorrow)
from BEAUTIFUL

ALTO SAX

Words and Music by GERRY GOFFIN
and CAROLE KING

WITH ONE LOOK

from SUNSET BOULEVARD

ALTO SAX

Music by ANDREW LLOYD WEBBER
Lyrics by DON BLACK and CHRISTOPHER HAMPTON,
with contributions by AMY POWERS

WRITTEN IN THE STARS

from Elton John and Tim Rice's AIDA

ALTO SAX

Music by ELTON JOHN
Lyrics by TIM RICE

YOU RULE MY WORLD

from THE FULL MONTY

ALTO SAX

Words and Music by
DAVID YAZBEK

YOU'LL NEVER WALK ALONE

from CAROUSEL

ALTO SAX

Lyrics by OSCAR HAMMERSTEIN II
Music by RICHARD RODGERS

YOU'LL BE IN MY HEART

Disney Presents TARZAN The Broadway Musical

ALTO SAX

Words and Music by
PHIL COLLINS

D.S. al Coda

CODA

YOU'VE GOT A FRIEND
from BEAUTIFUL

ALTO SAX

Words and Music by
CAROLE KING

Moderately

YOUNGER THAN SPRINGTIME
from SOUTH PACIFIC

ALTO SAX

Lyrics by OSCAR HAMMERSTEIN II
Music by RICHARD RODGERS